GEORGE MARTIN

HEALING:
reflections on the Gospel

Servant Books
Ann Arbor, Michigan

also by George Martin:

*Reading Scripture
As the Word of God*

*Parish Renewal:
A Charismatic Approach*

copyright © 1977 by George Martin

*Published by Servant Books
P.O. Box 617
Ann Arbor, Michigan 48107*

Scripture quotations in this book are from the following:

The Jerusalem Bible, copyright © 1966 by Darton, Longman & Todd, Ltd. and Doubleday & Company, Inc. and used by permission of the publisher.

The Revised Standard Version Bible
Copyrighted 1946, 1952, © 1971, 1973 by the Division of Christian Education of the National Council of the Churches of Christ in the U.S.A. and used by permission.

Printed in the United States of America

ISBN 0-89283-043-3

CONTENTS

Introduction	5
1. The Work of Jesus	12
2. Healing in the Church	22
3. Attitudes toward Healing	30
4. Faith for Healing	40
5. Resurrection	54

INTRODUCTION

They brought the boy to him and when the spirit saw him, immediately it convulsed the boy, and he fell on the ground and rolled about, foaming at the mouth. And Jesus asked his father, "How long has he had this?" And he said, "From childhood. And it has often cast him into the fire and into the water, to destroy him; but if you can do anything, have pity on us and help us." And Jesus said to him, "If you can! All things are possible to him who believes." Immediately the father of the child cried out and said, "I believe; help my unbelief!"

Mark 9:20-24

6   Healing: Reflections on the Gospel

Our hearts go out to the father of this afflicted boy. From childhood his son had been a victim of painful convulsions. The father could only watch helplessly each time his son was assailed, and wait for the attack to pass, hoping that his son would survive it, living in the fear that he would not.

The spirit that afflicted the boy was not content to merely throw him into convulsions. The spirit also cast him into fire and into water, burning him painfully, nearly drowning him. He was always in danger of death.

The language of Mark's Gospel indicates that the affliction had lasted many years: "From childhood" the son had been tormented. It would appear then that the son was no longer a mere child, at least in years. He should have been growing into manhood, working beside his father to learn his trade. Instead he was still a totally dependent child needing the constant care and protection of his father.

Luke's Gospel tells us that this son was an only child, making the affliction doubly tragic. The father must have worried about the future. Who would protect his son and care for him after he the father had died? Or if he survived into old age, who would take up the son's normal role of caring for him?

No doubt the father had explored every means that medicine offered to bring relief to his son. Would any parent do less? But medicine proved incapable of dealing with the root of the disease. And the father explored whatever healing might be had through religion. He consulted the disciples of Jesus, begging them to cast out the spirit that was destroying his son. No doubt he had previously brought his son to the priests of the temple, hoping that they would be able to restore his son to health. But all proved powerless against the affliction.

Thus the father did not just bring a sick son to Jesus for healing. He brought along years of suffering and frustration and near despair. When he came to Jesus, he did not merely bring someone he loved, someone he wished to see set free from a power that was destroying his life. He brought along his whole life and future also, focused as it was on his only child. He did not merely ask Jesus to have pity on his son; he asked Jesus to have pity "on us."

The father did not approach Jesus with an assured and easy faith. His attitude contrasts sharply with the centurion's, who confidently told Jesus that there was no need for him to visit his house: "only say the word, and my servant will be healed" (Matt. 8:8). The father's expectations were very tentative: "if you can do anything, have pity on us." Did faith or desperation bring the father to Jesus? Was Jesus simply one more in a long succession of possible remedies—all of which had failed in the past?

Jesus noticed the father's unbelief, but was very gentle with him. Who could blame a man for having little hope when his hopes had been so thoroughly disappointed in the past? Who could blame a man for having little faith when his every act of faith had gone unrewarded? Yet Jesus does ask faith of him: "All things are possible to him who believes."

The father of the child answered with a cry that is echoed in many hearts: "I believe; help my unbelief." Not a cry of confident faith—but neither a cry of despair. A cry of faith seeking assurance; a cry of a weak man wanting to be strong. A cry admitting unbelief, but begging to be delivered from it. A cry of wanting to believe—and believing.

Few of us are so sorely afflicted as this son and his father. Most of the sicknesses which strike our family are mercifully less severe and less prolonged. Yet most of us probably are acquainted with persons who suffer greatly: those who are gravely ill, who are undergoing major surgery, or who are afflicted with a long-term disability. Perhaps our own family even has been touched by such pain.

Whatever the seriousness of the illness or injury, our hearts go out to those who are struck down—our children, our parents, our friends, our relatives. We have sympathy not only for the one afflicted, but for those nearest who are also affected.

We are concerned that the ill and injured receive the best help medical science can give them. Yet despite the sophistication of modern medicine, we know that there is much it cannot do. There are disabilities it cannot relieve; there are healings it cannot bring; there are pains it cannot ease. In our concern for those we know who are sick, we want a more thorough healing for them than any human doctor can give.

We therefore turn to God in prayer, asking Him to bring a thorough healing, a rapid healing, a healing beyond human hope. But our prayer is often like the prayer of the boy's father: "If you can do anything..." We turn to God with doubts and uncertainties. Can this illness be healed? Will healing come if I pray? What if I pray and nothing happens? Does God want to cure this illness? Do my prayers really make any difference?

Nonetheless, we pray, or attempt to pray. Our words may be halting and inarticulate. We may wonder if we are only turning to God in desperation. We pray, remembering all the times in the past when we never gave him a thought, or thanked him for the health our family did enjoy. We may be very conscious that we are not very good at praying, particularly at praying for a healing. We may have the feeling that we are praying without much faith—perhaps with no faith at all.

We have heard the words of Jesus: "All things are possible to him who believes." Yet those words do not make our belief any easier or firmer. For some they are even the cause of great guilt: "My loved one is still sick because I do not have enough faith." Many of us can only muster the mixed faith of the father: "I believe; help my unbelief."

Yet that is all Jesus demands of us. He surely invites us to a greater faith—but he does not demand of us the impossible. He invited the father of the afflicted son to greater faith—but he healed his son despite his doubts. He knew that the father had put his whole life into that cry, "I believe; help my unbelief." He accepted that life as brought before him and placed at his feet, despite the unbelief and weakness in the father's cry.

Perhaps Jesus even had special compasssion on the father precisely because he was weak and doubting. "Those who are well have no need of a physician, but those who are sick" (Luke 5:31). Jesus came to bring us God's life and strength, not to demand it of us. "God shows his love for us in that while we were yet sinners Christ died for us" (Rom. 5:8). He loved us to free us from our weakness and doubts; he loved us because our weakness and doubts needed his love to be healed.

Jesus has the same compassion for us today that he had for the father and his afflicted son. He will honor our imperfect faith, just as he honored the imperfect faith of that father. He will invite our belief to grow; he wants belief to replace our unbelief. But he will first welcome our lives brought before him and placed at his feet—despite our weaknesses and doubts, despite our hesitations and failings.

Jesus invites us today to bring our sick before him, to pray for those who are ill and afflicted, to turn to him for healing. No less today than when he walked the earth, he wishes to bring a complete healing to man, a healing of body and spirit.

1

THE WORK OF JESUS

As we read through the gospel accounts, we are struck by the number of times Jesus healed someone. Mark's Gospel—probably the first gospel to be written—describes in its first chapter the beginnings of Jesus' public ministry. Jesus cures a demoniac at Capernaum (Mark 1:23-27), and then visits Simon's house. "Now Simon's mother-in-law had gone to bed with fever, and they told him about her straightaway. He went to her, took her by the hand and helped her up. And the fever left her and she began to wait on them" (Mark 1:29-31). A seemingly commonplace cure—so she could fix supper for them!

Chapter one of Mark's Gospel goes on to describe how those who were sick and possessed by devils were brought to Jesus: "The whole town came crowding round the door, and he cured many who were suffering from diseases of one kind or another" (Mark 1:33-34). The next day, a leper came to him "and pleaded on his knees: 'If you want to' he said 'you can cure me.' Feeling sorry for him, Jesus stretched out his hands and touched him. 'Of course I want to!' he said. 'Be cured!' And the leprosy left him at once and he was cured" (Mark 1:40-42).

These incidents from the first chapter of Mark's Gospel are typical of all four gospel narratives of the life of Jesus. Even a hasty reading of the gospels reveals that healing was an integral part of the mission and ministry of Jesus. Crowds flocked to Jesus seeking healing—so much so that he sometimes had to slip away quietly to find the peace to pray. And it was Jesus' healings that infuriated his enemies as much as anything: "The chief priests and Pharisees called a meeting. 'Here is this man working all these signs' they said 'and what action are we taking?'" (John 11:47).

The cure of the leper described in Mark 1 contains the keynote of the entire healing ministry of Jesus. Those who came to Jesus for healing were healed. Never do the gospels record that Jesus refused to heal someone who asked to be healed. Rather, Jesus' attitude was "Of course I want to heal you!" And when Jesus said "Be healed," they were healed.

When Jesus had to describe his own ministry, he spoke in terms of both the message that he taught and the healings that he performed:

> Now John in his prison heard what Christ was doing and he sent his disciples to ask him, "Are you the one who is to come, or have we got to wait for someone else?" Jesus answered, "Go back and tell John what you hear and see; the blind see again, the lame walk, lepers are cleansed, and the deaf hear, and the dead are raised to life and the Good News is proclaimed to the poor; and happy is the man who does not lose faith in me."
>
> Matt. 11:2-6

John asked the fundamental question of belief: are you the Messiah? Are you the one sent by God that we are waiting for? Jesus in response did not simply say yes, but pointed to his public ministry. His answer was, in effect, "Yes, I am the Messiah—and I am carrying out the mission of the Messiah. I am bringing health to the sick, sight to the blind, Good News to the poor. These works you see me do are the works of the Messiah sent by God."

Jesus did not conceive his mission in completely "otherworldly" terms. He did not come to save men's souls, but to save men. He did not come merely to proclaim the Good News that God is love, but to demonstrate it in action. He brought healing from sickness as well as from sin; he brought health for the whole man.

After Jesus' ascension to heaven, the Apostles were filled with the power of the Spirit to proclaim that Jesus Christ was the savior of the world. The emphasis in their sermons was often more on what Jesus did than what Jesus said. On Pentecost day, Peter spoke to the crowd: "Men of Israel, listen to what I am going to say: Jesus the Nazarene was a man commended to you by God by the miracles and portents and signs that God worked through him when he was among you, as you all know" (Acts 2:22). And later, when Peter wanted to instruct Cornelius the centurion about Jesus, he told him that "God had anointed him with the Holy Spirit and with power, and because God was with him, Jesus went about doing good and curing all who had fallen into the power of the devil" (Acts 10:38). The Apostles who walked with Jesus certainly viewed healing as an important part of his ministry.

The mission and ministry of Jesus was not limited to healing. His teaching was an essential aspect of his work, and he performed miracles other than healing. But curing the sick was a very prominent part of the public ministry of

Jesus Christ—too prominent to be dismissed as incidental or unimportant.

When we examine how Jesus healed, we are struck by the great variety of ways in which he restored people to health. Often Jesus touched the sick, or laid his hands upon them (see Matt. 8:3 and Luke 13:13, for example). Sometimes sick people reached out to touch him, or even merely touch the fringe of his cloak, "and all those who touched it were completely cured" (Matt. 14:36). Sometimes there was no physical contact between Jesus and the sick person at all; sometimes a word or command from Jesus was all that was necessary (see Mark 3:5 and Luke 5:24, for example). Sometimes the gospels describe no contact or command of Jesus, but only tell us that the person was healed (as in Luke 7:1-10, for example).

Jesus did not always use the same method even in curing the same disease. One blind man he healed instantly by a word (Luke 18:42); another received his sight back by stages (Mark 8:22-26). Still another was healed after Jesus made a paste with spittle, and covered his eyes with it (John 9:6). Jesus asked some people to make a profession of faith (Matthew 9:28); other times he did not (Mark 8:22-26). Sometimes Jesus healed in response to the pleas of the blind (Matt. 20:29-34) or their friends (Mark 8:22), but sometimes Jesus healed simply to demonstrate the love of God. Jesus gave sight to one blind man at his own initiative, without being asked (John 9:1-7).

Many healings by Jesus took place in the midst of a crowd—such as that of the paralytic lowered down through the roof (Mark 2:1-12). Other healings were deliberately done in private. Jesus took one blind man apart from the crowd to heal him, and told him to go directly home afterwards without going back into the village (Mark 8:22-26).

Jesus often instructed the cured person to tell no one about what happened to him: "Then Jesus sternly warned them, 'Take care that no one learns about this' " (Matt. 9:30). Jesus sometimes even gave this instruction when it seemed impossible to keep the healing a secret. A crowd had gathered outside the house of Jairus to mourn the death of his daughter. Jesus restored her to life, but afterwards, he ordered her parents not to let anyone know about it—despite the obvious difficulty in keeping such a marvel from the friends and relatives gathered outside (Mark 5:38-43). Yet on other occasions, Jesus' instructions were just the opposite: "Go back home and report all that God has done for you" (Luke 8:39).

If the manner in which Jesus healed varied, so did the cause he ascribed to the illness. Most often, the gospels do not tell us what caused the sickness or infirmity that Jesus healed. Sometimes, however, the affliction was the result of an evil spirit, and the person was healed when Jesus cast out that spirit. Two examples are, the boy brought by his father (Mark 9:20) and the woman bent double for 18 years (Luke 13:10-17). Sometimes the sickness seemed to be connected with sin, and Jesus' healing involved a healing from sin as well as from infirmity. Jesus first told the paralytic brought to him, "Your sins are forgiven" and then "Get up and walk" (Matt. 9:1-7). After he healed the man lying by the pool, he warned him. "Now that you are well again, be sure not to sin any more or something worse may happen to you" (John 5:14).

Yet in other cases, Jesus clearly teaches that the sickness was not caused by the sins of the afflicted person. " 'Rabbi, who sinned, this man or his parents, for him to have been born blind?' 'Neither he nor his parents sinned,' Jesus answered 'he was born blind so that the works of God might be displayed in him' " (John 9:2-3). Thus we see that sometimes the sickness had a meaning in the plan of God. Jesus allowed his close friend Lazarus to die so that his release from death might increase the faith of the disciples (John 11:15).

An important element in the cures worked by Jesus was the faith of the sick person or his friends. But even here, we see a variety of situa-

The Work of Jesus 19

tions, and cannot impose an oversimplified theory on the gospel accounts.

In some instances, the faith of the sick played an important role in their being healed. The woman with a hemorrhage who approached Jesus in a crowd and touched his cloak did so in faith, and was cured at that instant. Jesus then asked, "Who touched me?" He knew someone had been healed, but he did not know who it was. After discovering it was the woman, he told her "your faith has restored you to health" (Luke 8:43-48). In this incident, Jesus did not seek out the sick person, and he was not even aware of her presence before she was cured. Her faith in approaching Jesus was responsible for her restoration to health.

Sometimes the gospels do not describe the faith of the sick person, but talk about the faith of their friends. When some men brought a paralytic to Jesus, Jesus saw their faith and healed the paralytic in response (Luke 5:17-25). When a centurion came to Jesus and asked that he heal his servant, Jesus marveled at his faith and the servant was healed (Luke 7:1-10). The gospel says nothing about the faith of the paralytic or the servant—they were healed in response to the faith of others.

When Jesus encountered a positive lack of faith, it limited the works that he could perform. The people in his home town would only accept him as "the carpenter, the son of Mary" and Mark's Gospel tells us that "he could work no miracle there, though he cured a few sick people by laying his hands on them. He was amazed at their lack of faith" (Mark 6:1-6).

It would be a mistake, however, to believe that Jesus demanded faith before he would heal, or that he could not heal someone who did not have faith in him. The sick man lying by the pool with five porticos had been ill for 38 years. Yet when Jesus asked him whether he wanted to be well again, the man's only reply was to make an excuse why he hadn't been healed in the past. He did not ask Jesus to heal him; he did not even directly say that he wanted to be healed. Yet Jesus healed him. Even after his healing, he did not know who Jesus was. When he was asked who had healed him, he had no idea who it was (John 5:1-13). Jesus healed this man without requiring any faith on his part—without requiring that the sick man acknowledge him as the Messiah or even directly ask him for healing.

Sometimes Jesus did ask for faith in his power to heal. He asked the two blind men who followed after him, "Do you believe I can do this?" (Matt. 9:28). But sometimes faith did not seem to enter into the picture at all. When Jesus was in the Gerasene district and saw a man possessed by devils, he cast out the devils and healed him—despite the man's inability to exercise faith (Luke 8:26-36).

The Work of Jesus   21

Nor did faith necessarily result from the healings Jesus performed. When word spread that Jesus had healed the possessed man, "the entire population of the Gerasene territory was in a state of panic and asked Jesus to leave them. So he got back into the boat and went back" (Luke 8:37). This was hardly a reaction of faith! When John sent messengers to ask if Jesus was the Messiah, Jesus told them to "Go back and tell John what you have seen and heard: the blind see again, the lame walk, lepers are cleansed, and the deaf hear, the dead are raised to life, the Good News is proclaimed to the poor and *happy is the man who does not lose faith in me"* (Luke 7:22-23). The very signs and wonders which should be occasions of faith can also be a source of confusion and scandal.

It is clear that healing played a major role in the public ministry of Jesus. We cannot believe in Jesus on his own terms without coming to grips with his own description of his ministry. "Am I the Messiah? Look at what I do: the deaf hear, the blind see, the lame walk."

Nor can we reduce Jesus to a mere wonder worker, a man walking around with a simple magic formula for health. The variety and complexity of his healings are too great to allow us to make them the object of our veneration. We must focus our eyes on him who performed the healings—not on the healings themselves.

2

HEALING IN THE CHURCH

Not only did Jesus heal the sick who came to him; he commissioned his apostles to do the same. "He called the Twelve together and gave them power and authority over all devils and to cure diseases, and he sent them out to proclaim the kingdom of God and to heal ... So they set out and went from village to village proclaiming the Good News and healing everywhere" (Luke 9:1-2, 6).

Nor was the ministry of healing to be exercised only by the twelve Apostles; the disciples were also authorized to heal in his name. "After this the Lord appointed seventy-two others and

Healing in the Church 23

sent them out ahead of him . . . 'Whenever you go into a town where they make you welcome, eat what is set before you. Cure those in it who are sick, and say, "The kingdom of God is very near to you" ' " (Luke 10:1, 8-9).

Jesus not only sent out his followers to heal the sick; he expected that they would be able to do it. He rejoiced when they brought back reports of their success (Luke 10:17-20), and he expressed his disappointment when they failed (Matt. 17:14-20).

Before Jesus ascended into heaven, he commissioned his apostles to preach the gospel to the whole world. One of the marks of those who believed in the Good News was to be their authority to heal: "They will lay their hands on the sick, who will recover " (Mark 16:18).

It is no surprise, then, that the healing of the sick was one of the characteristics of the Church from its earliest days. After Pentecost, Peter and John were on their way to the Temple to pray. A cripple at the door of the temple begged them for money. Instead Peter said to him, "I have neither silver nor gold, but I will give you what I have: in the name of Jesus Christ the Nazarene, walk!" (Acts 3:6). When the cripple began "walking and jumping and praising God," everyone was astonished. But Peter asked them, "Why are you so surprised at this? . . . It is the name of Jesus which, through our faith in it, has brought back the strength of this man ..." (Acts 3:12, 16). Peter acted as if healing in the name of Jesus was to be considered a normal occurrence in the life of the Church.

This cure of a cripple brought the early Christians to the attention of the Jewish authorities, who arrested Peter and John for questioning. But the authorities were at a loss to know what to do, knowing that "It is obvious to everybody in Jerusalem that a miracle has been worked through them in public, and we cannot deny it" (Acts 4:16).

After their release, Peter and John continued to heal the sick. "So many signs and wonders were worked among the people at the hands of the apostles that the sick were even taken out into the streets and laid on beds and sleeping-mats in the hope that at least the shadow of Peter might fall across some of them as he went past. People even came crowding in from the towns round about Jerusalem, bringing with them their sick and those tormented by unclean spirits, and all of them were cured" (Acts 5:12, 15-16).

It was this ministry of healing that once again earned imprisonment for the apostles (Acts 5:17-18), and it was this ministry of healing that demonstrated the presence of the power of God in the Church. As in the time of Jesus' public ministry, healing was not limited to the apostles.

Stephen was ordained as deacon to "wait on tables," but was also "filled with grace and power and began to work miracles and great signs among the people" (Acts 6:8). Philip, another deacon, preached the gospel in Samaria with great effectiveness because the people "heard of the miracles he worked or because they saw them for themselves . . . several paralytics and cripples were cured" (Acts 8:6-8).

Paul also healed. "Seeing that the man had the faith to be cured, Paul said in a loud voice, 'Get to your feet—stand up', and the cripple jumped up and began to walk" (Acts 14:9-10). In fact, "so remarkable were the miracles worked by God at Paul's hands that handkerchiefs or aprons which touched him were taken to the sick, and they were cured of their illnesses, and the evil spirits came out of them" (Acts 19:11-12).

As in the ministry of Jesus, the early Church brought God's healing in many ways. Sometimes the healing took place at the words of an apostle: "Peter said to him, 'Aeneas, Jesus Christ cures you: get up and fold up your sleeping mat'" (Acts 9:34). Sometimes hands were laid upon the sick person, as when Ananias laid hands upon Paul for his eyesight to return (Acts 9:17). Sometimes the shadow of an apostle, or a handkerchief he had touched, was the occasion of healing (Acts 5:15 and 19:11).

Sometimes those who were sick sought out the apostles, coming to them with faith that they could be healed in the name of Jesus Christ. But sometimes it is evident that the afflicted person did not have faith. When Paul and Silas were in Philippi, they were followed around by a possessed girl who kept shouting, "Here are the servants of the most high God." After a few days this got on Paul's nerves: "She did this every day until Paul lost his temper one day and turned around and said to the spirit, 'I order you in the name of Jesus Christ to leave that woman.' The spirit went out of her then and there," and Paul was bothered by her no more—a healing because Paul ran out of patience! (Acts 16:17-18).

The authority over sickness granted to the apostles extended even to death itself. Peter brought back to life a woman who was well beloved in the early Church for the many good works she performed. Soon after her death, Peter knelt by her side and prayed, and then commanded her to arise. This dramatic healing was the occasion for many coming to faith in Jesus Christ (Acts 9:36-42).

Paul also raised a dead person to life—but in circumstances that have their wry humor. On Paul's last journey to Jerusalem, he stopped by Troas to visit the Christian community in that city. On the night before he was to leave, the community assembled to listen to his words of farewell. Paul did not disappoint their expectations: "he preached a sermon that went on till the middle of the night." However, a tragedy struck: "As Paul went on and on, a young man called Eutychus who was sittting on a window-sill grew drowsy and was overcome by sleep and fell to the ground three floors below. He was picked up dead." Paul interrupted his sermon long enough to go downstairs and restore the boy to life. "Then he went back upstairs where he broke bread and ate and carried on talking till he left at daybreak"—an all-night sermon that Paul would not even allow death to interrupt! (Acts 20:7-12).

From the earliest days of the Church, healing accompanied the preaching of the gospel. "The many miracles and signs worked through the apostles made a deep impression on everyone" (Acts 2:43). And at the end of the book of Acts, there is still healing: during Paul's stopover on the island of Malta on his journey to Rome, "Publius' father was in bed suffering from feverish attacks and dysentery. Paul went in to see him, and after a prayer he laid his hands on the man and healed him. When this happened, the other sick people on the island came as well and were cured" (Acts 28:8-9). Whenever the gospel was preached, "the Lord supported all they said about his gift of grace, allowing signs and wonders to be performed by them" (Acts 14:3).

Healing was a normal part of the life of the early Church. It was not something that happened only on rare occasions; it was not something that happened only when a very select group of people prayed. It happened commonly and was part of the experience of the Christian community. When Paul wrote to the Galatians, he could remind them that God had freely given them the Spirit and "worked miracles in their midst" because they had believed the message he had preached to them (Gal. 3:5).

This is not to say that every dead person was raised to life, or every sick person healed. It is to say that healing was an integral aspect of the life of the early Church. It was expected, as a sign of God's love for his people.

Healing has never been absent from the life of the Church. In every age, in one place or another, healing has marked the ministry of great men of God. The superabundance of healing that was present in the early Church has often been absent. But the healing power of God has never been quenched; works of healing have never completely disappeared from the life of the Church.

For example, Augustine, writing in the fifth century, could state that he knew of cures past counting taking place in his time. He mentions

Healing in the Church 29

in his book, *The City of God*, that in his own diocese of Hippo alone, nearly seventy attested miracles were recorded in a two-year period.

There is a resurgence of belief in the healing power of prayer today. Around the world, Christians are discovering that God does hear and honor their prayers for the sick and suffering. Healing is once again becoming an expected part of life in the Body of Christ. As our faith in the healing power of God increases, God increasingly honors that faith by his works of healing.

We should respond to the healing presence of God in the world by praying for the healing that he offers. We are called to "put on the mind of Christ" with regard to healing—to bring our attitudes in line with God's revelation about healing. And we are invited to pray in faith for God's healing power to be released in our midst, touching us, touching those we love.

3

ATTITUDES TOWARD HEALING

Our attitudes toward sickness and health will influence how we pray to God for healing. If we believe that God is indifferent to our suffering, we probably won't pray to him for healing. If we believe that we will be cured every time we are sick, if we simply have enough faith, we will pray quite differently—but we may feel condemned those times we are not healed. Without attempting to present a full treatment of all the questions, I would like to recommend the following attitudes toward healing:

1. *God wants man to enjoy health.* God's

Attitudes Toward Healing 31

plan at creation was for man to enjoy physical and emotional health; it was through sin that sickness and death entered into the world (Gen. 3:16-19).

Jesus Christ came to restore what man had lost through sin. Jesus came not only to bring forgiveness of sin, but also to repair the evil effects of sin. Jesus came to bring salvation to us as complete individuals, not only to bring salvation for our souls. He came to bring us "abundant life" (John 10:10), the beginnings of which we should experience here and now. The healings Jesus worked were not merely signs of his divinity; they were also part of his mission of restoring man to his wholeness in the image of God.

We instinctively desire to be healthy, and usually do whatever we can to get well when we are ill. We consider it natural and normal to take medicine when we are sick, or to go to a doctor. We rarely have to sit down and deliberate whether we want to get well or not; we instinctively want to be healthy. In the same way, we should as a rule expect that God's desire for us is for us to be healthy. We should not automatically assume that sickness we experience is a cross sent to us by God, to be borne with patience. We should rather understand sickness as an evil, something that it is normal to want to remove from our lives.

Just as we turn to doctors and medicine when we are sick, so should we turn to God in prayer. We should pray for healing: healing for ourselves and others when we are sick, healing from whatever kind of sickness afflicts us. We should consider it natural and normal to pray for healing, just as we consider it natural and normal to take medicine. We should have no more hesitation in praying for healing than we do in taking aspirin for a headache.

Jesus does ask us to carry our cross in imitation of him. There is a mystery of redemptive suffering, and illness or infirmity can be part of it. But the cross that Jesus normally asks us to carry is the cross of dying to ourselves by laying down our lives in love. We should not assume that every sickness is a cross we are asked to carry. Rather, unless we have very good and specific reasons to believe otherwise, we should assume that God desires us to be well and we should pray to be well.

There is a time appointed for each person to die. Death, brought into the world through man's sin, is ultimately vanquished only through our resurrection in Christ. There is a time to pray for someone's healing from sickness; there is a time to pray for someone's peaceful death and joyful resurrection into eternal life. A person's age and the circumstances of his life should guide us in praying for them as we ought.

Attitudes Toward Healing 33

However, our basic attitude should be one of seeking health: health for ourselves, health for others. Our basic attitude should be to view sickness as one of the evils that Jesus came to free us from. We should normally expect that God's will for us is health, and turn to him in prayer to ask him for that health.

2. *We should use every natural means at our disposal to care for our health.* We should preserve our health through wise and temperate living. We should use medical science to restore our health when we are sick.

God's healing power in our lives must never become an excuse for us to abuse our health. We should take responsibility for preserving our health through proper nutrition, exercise, and rest, avoiding whatever we know to be harmful to ourselves.

If we are chronically fatigued and lack the energy to get our work done, we perhaps should pray for a healing from this condition. But perhaps we should also examine our lifestyle. Am I eating a well-balanced diet? Do I get enough exercise? Do I get enough rest at night? God does not want to make up for our junk food meals, our laziness, our staying up late at night to watch TV. He wants us to correct these bad patterns of life so that we might enjoy good health as a natural result of the way we live.

Similarly, we can also abuse our health by

imprudence—driving ourselves to take on too many responsibilities or make more money, by not seeking medical attention when we should, by our excessive worry about tomorrow, and so forth. God's desire that we be healthy is first of all a desire that we correct those conditions in our life which lead to bad health. We should pray for the strength of will to overcome bad habits, rather than for a divine healing from the consequences of bad habits.

If we do find ourselves sick, then we should use whatever means medical science can offer to restore our health. Belief in the healing power of prayer does not mean disbelief in the healing power of medicine and doctors. No one should create a false opposition between God healing us through the natural means of medical science and his healing in answer to prayer. We should use medicine and pray for healing at the same time.

There is no contradiction between reliance on medicine and reliance on God; medicines are part of God's plan for our health. Paul advised Timothy to "use a little wine for the sake of your stomach and your frequent ailments" (1 Tim. 5:23). Whatever the medicinal value of wine may be, Paul prescribed it as something helpful to Timothy's health. In effect, he urged Timothy to make use of a "medicine"; he did not command Timothy to rely on prayer alone.

Attitudes Toward Healing 35

In the gospel accounts of Jesus' healings of lepers, Jesus always instructed them to "go and show yourself to the priest and make the offering for your healing as Moses prescribed it, as evidence for them" (Luke 5:14; see also Luke 17:14). Under the Law of Moses, the priest performed a role similar to that of a public health doctor today: he would certify whether someone was or was not a leper, and consequently whether they had to be quarantined from the community in order to prevent an epidemic from breaking out (Lev. 13, 14). When Jesus sent the healed lepers to the priest, he was submitting his healings to the examination and judgment of those who had the authority to diagnose this type of sickness.

Today, those who believe themselves healed by God should likewise submit themselves to doctors. It should be the doctor's role to diagnose sickness and certify health. If someone believes that they have been healed through prayer, they should present themselves to their doctor for their healing to be confirmed. Normally, no one should stop taking any prescribed medications except at their doctor's orders. Medication should be discontinued when the need for it is gone; the best judge of that need will be the physician who prescribed the medication.

3. *There is much about healing that we do*

not understand. Healing is largely a mystery. This does not mean that we should cease praying for healing with expectant faith. However, it does mean that we must be very careful not to impose our own ideas on the mystery of God's plan for us, or to limit our understanding of his love for us. We cannot reduce God's healing power to a magical formula.

Our examination of the New Testament accounts of healing revealed the mysterious nature of God's sovereign action. We found no sure formula for healing, no magical technique for restoring health. We found only the power of God mediated through Jesus Christ. Jesus healed in a great variety of ways: sometimes he spoke a word; sometimes he laid hands upon a person; sometimes he healed at a great distance. His healings often occurred instantaneously, but sometimes they took time. Jesus usually required faith for healing, but again, not always. Jesus himself was the only constant factor in the many healings he performed.

God granted Paul remarkable healing gifts, even the power to raise the dead to life. Yet Paul once had to leave one of his co-workers, Trophimus, behind "ill at Miletus" while he went on ahead (2 Tim. 4:20). Presumably Paul had prayed for Trophimus to be cured of his illness so that he could travel with him—yet Trophimus was not immediately healed. Presumably too

Attitudes Toward Healing 37

Paul had prayed with Timothy for his health—yet Timothy was still subject to "frequent ailments" (1 Tim. 5:23). Yet such experiences did not discourage Paul from continuing to pray for the sick.

Paul himself experienced sickness. An apparently prolonged and unpleasant illness forced him to interrupt one of his journeys for an unexpected stay in Galatia (Gal. 4:12-14). If Paul could heal others, why could he not always heal himself? If healing gifts were present in the Church at Galatia, why was not Paul prayed with and healed forthwith, and sent on his way?

Healing through prayer is not something magical. Healing is a sovereign action of God; it does not happen because we utter the right words or perform just the right action. When we pray to God for healing, we submit to his will; we do not seek to control him through our prayer or faith. Nor should we condemn ourselves if our prayer is apparently not answered. There is more to God's plan than we can grasp; there is a mystery to healing that we cannot fathom.

4. *We should focus on the "healing" aspect of what the Lord does, and not on its "spectacular" aspects.* If God wished to astonish men with extraordinary miracles, he could perform signs and wonders in the heavens. The healings experienced in our daily lives are important

because they are manifestations of God's love for us and an invitation to greater faith and thanksgiving. When we pray for healing, we pray primarily in order to get well, not primarily for God to work a wonder. The healing we receive is significant more because it frees us from sickness than because it is a dazzling display of God's power over the laws of nature.

There is a need for the miraculous in the Church, and we need to be rigorous in our criteria of what is miraculous and what is not. But the focus in most instances of healing should be different: not that a miracle has (or has not) occurred, but that a person has been restored to health. We can rejoice when someone has been freed from the debilitating effects of sickness without being certain whether the cure came entirely from supernatural causes or not. We can have our faith built up by healings which do not fulfill the rigorous requirements demanded of proven miracles.

It thus matters little whether the sickness we are freed from is rooted in organic or psychosomatic disorder. Any sickness is sickness; any healing from God can be received in faith as a manifestation of his love for us. It matters little whether our healing occurs suddenly or gradually, whether it is the result of a sovereign act of God or accomplished in conjunction with the use of medication and therapy. And in most cases it matters little whether medical science can document that a miracle has occured or not. By their nature, many sicknesses do not lend themselves to such documentation.

What does matter is that God is present among us, extending his healing touch to us, inviting us to rejoice in his life for us, inviting us to grow in faith and trust in him. What does matter is that we are restored to health, and grow in our faith-filled reliance on God our Father.

4

FAITH FOR HEALING

"Seeing that the man had the faith to be cured, Paul said to him in a loud voice, 'Get to your feet—stand up,' and the cripple jumped up and began to walk" (Acts 14:9-10). Our faith plays a role in God's healing power becoming manifest in our midst. But our faith is sometimes very weak. Our faith is often like the faith of the man who brought his possessed son to Jesus: "I believe—help my unbelief."

"Faith is the assurance of things hoped for, the conviction of things unseen" (Heb. 11:1). What we hold by faith are precisely those truths

Faith for Healing 41

that we would not know by experience or reason alone. What we hold by faith are those truths that have been revealed to us by Jesus Christ. Our faith for healing must rest upon the revelation made in Christ Jesus. The faith we have for healing must be the faith that Jesus invites us to have.

Jesus taught many things about God during his years of public ministry, and gave commandments that his disciples were to follow. But the most important truth about God that he revealed was that God is our Father, and his most important instruction was that we are to have the kind of relationship with our heavenly Father that children ideally have with their earthly fathers.

Jesus claimed that God was his own Father; he prayed to him as his Father. To us today it might seem natural that Jesus should address God this way, but the contemporaries of Jesus must have been startled to hear him talk about God as his Father. In the whole of the Old Testament, there are only about 15 references to God as Father—and these are generally references to God as Father of the whole Chosen People. Jesus, however, constantly referred to God as *his* Father. The gospels contain over 150 instances of Jesus talking about God as his Father, or addressing him in prayer as Father.

Jesus' claim that the God of Abraham, the

God of Isaac, the God of Jacob was his Father revealed an essential aspect of his identity and mission. Jesus walked among us as the Son of God. And he was not the Son in some vague or distant sense; he was a son intimately related to the Father, a son on terms of complete familiarity with his Father.

Mark's Gospel recounts Jesus' prayer in the garden of Gethsemane in these words: " 'Abba (Father)' he said, 'Everything is possible for you. Take his cup away from me. But let it be as you, not I would have it' " (Mark 14:36). The word "abba" is an Aramaic word, Aramaic being the language Jesus spoke. The gospels as we have them were written in Greek; "abba" is one of the few Aramaic words of Jesus preserved for us. But it is a very significant word.

"Abba" is the word a young child would use in addressing his father. The origins of the word lie in the babbling sounds made by an infant: "dada, mama, papa, abba." At the time of Jesus, older sons and daughters could refer to their fathers as "abba"—but the connotations stemming from the origins of the word were never lost. If we were to look for an English equivalent for "abba" today, "daddy" would be a more accurate translation than the formal word "father."

Jesus in his prayers addressed God as "abba"—almost "daddy." While his prayers deeply reverenced and worshiped God, they did address God in a very intimate and familiar way. Jesus prayed not to a distant God but to a close and loving "abba." Jesus spoke to his heavenly father with the simplicity and intimacy of a small child speaking to his earthly father.

Were Jesus not the Son of God, such intimacy would have been blasphemous. No mere man could take it upon himself to address God as "abba"—to approach the creator of the universe with the same informality a small child has with its father.

Yet this is precisely what Jesus invites us to do:

> Now once as he was in a certain place praying, and when he had finished one of his disciples said, "Lord, teach us to pray, just as John taught his disciples." He said to them, "Say this when you pray: Father, may your name be held holy, your kingdom come . . ."
>
> Luke 11:1-2

The prayer that we say as the Lord's Prayer is the prayer that Jesus taught the disciples so that they could pray as he prayed—and it addresses God as "Father," as "Our Father."

Jesus did not merely teach us to pray to God as our Father; there is also evidence that he authorized his followers to use the same intimate address "abba" as he did. When Paul wished to describe the prayer of Christians, he employed the same Aramaic word that Jesus used:

> Everyone moved by the Spirit is a son of God. The spirit you received is not the spirit of slaves bringing fear into our lives again; it is the spirit of sons, and makes us cry out, "Abba, Father!"
>
> Rom. 8:14-15

> The proof that you are sons is that God has sent the Spirit of his Son into our hearts: the Spirit that cries "Abba, Father," and it is this that makes you a son.
>
> Gal. 4:6-7

When we pray as Jesus taught us to pray, we pray to God as our Father—as "Abba." We are not to approach God in fear; we are not slaves cringing before a master. Nor are we to approach God with uncertainty about whether he really cares for us. We can confidently approach our Father as his sons. Jesus Christ has given us great intimacy with God. His Holy Spirit dwelling within us has made us God's children.

Our prayer to the Father should be even more faith-filled and trusting than the centurion's request that Jesus heal his servant. The centurion respected Jesus as one who could cure his ser-

Faith for Healing 45

vant by a mere word; he had faith in Jesus' power over all things (Luke 7:1-10). But there is no evidence that the centurion was on terms of intimacy with Jesus. The centurion did not ask in the way a young child asks his father for what he needs; he asked as one man asks a more powerful man for a favor: he acknowledged Jesus' power and goodness, but asked without great familiarity or affection.

By contrast, our prayer to God must be based upon the fundamental reality that God has adopted us as his children. Our prayer must be a prayer to "our Father," asking him to "give us this day our daily bread" in all the forms that we need it. Our confidence in prayer stems from our praying to our Father:

> That is why I am telling you not to worry about your life and what you are to eat, nor about your body and how you are to clothe it ... Look at the birds in the sky. They do not sow or reap or gather into barns; yet your heavenly Father feeds them. Are you not worth much more than they are? ... So do not worry; do not say, "What are we to eat? What are we to drink? How are we to be clothed?" It is the pagans who set their hearts on all these things. Your heavenly Father knows you need them all.
>
> Matt. 6:25, 26, 31-32

Jesus takes pains to emphasize this point: we pray to God as our Father, and we pray with the confidence of children turning to their Father for their need.

So I say to you: Ask, and it will be given to you; search, and you will find; knock, and the door will be opened to you. For the one who asks always receives; the one who searches always finds; the one who knocks will always have the door opened to him. What father among you would hand his son a stone when he asked for bread? Or hand him a snake instead of a fish? Or hand him a scorpion if he asked for an egg? If you then, who are evil, know how to give your children what is good, how much more will your Father in heaven give good things to those who ask him.

Luke 11:9-13; cf. Matt. 7:7-11

Our prayer for healing is a turning to our Father in heaven, to ask him for health. Our attitude should be like that of a child, who asks his father for what he needs, asking with simplicity and trust, on the basis of the love he knows his father has for him. We too ask our heavenly Father for what we need—including health—on the basis of the love he has for us, because he has adopted us as his sons and daughters.

Faith for Healing   47

Healing comes from God, not from our prayer or our faith. We should not try to compose the perfect prayer for healing, or work ourselves up into a state of absolute certainty that God is going to heal in this particular circumstance. Rather, our part is simply to present our needs and desires to the Lord, relying on his love for us and his power to heal.

We may need courage to begin praying for healing. We may have to get over a feeling of awkwardness. If we are praying for someone else for the first time, we might begin by simply asking them whether they would like us to pray with them and for them. Their response will most often be one of real gratitude, giving us courage and encouragement.

We should spend a moment reflecting upon just what to pray for, silently asking God for the inspiration to be able to pray as we should. Sometimes we will be in doubt exactly what to pray for. We should simply acknowledge such doubts and seek God's guidance. In order to make our prayer for healing as specific as possible, we should spend a moment focusing on the form our prayer should take and on what we want to ask God to grant.

Our actual prayer should focus on God's love for the one who is sick—for ourselves or for another. We should ask that the person be restored to full health in the image of God. When we pray for people we love very much, we should draw strength from the realization that God's love for them is much greater than our own.

Our prayer should be positive, focusing on the health to be restored rather than upon the sickness and pain that is being suffered. We should acknowledge the presence of Jesus Christ as we pray, and invoke the redemption he has won for us. There are no magic words or phrases, no special tone of voice to use. Our prayer should sound like us, simply and sincerely asking our Father to do something, using what words come to our minds.

Our prayer should be marked by confidence and thanksgiving. Our confidence does not stem from our lack of doubts but from the love we know God has for us, or for the person we are praying for. Similarly, we base our thanksgiving not so much on a certitude that we know what the results of our prayer will be as on our gratitude that in Jesus Christ we have access to the Father.

Following the example of Jesus and the early Christians, prayer for healing is often accompanied by a laying on of hands. This traditional practice is a concrete expression of affection and concern. There is nothing magical about laying on of hands. If we are praying with someone who would be uncomfortable with this type of prayer, it might be best to simply pray for them while holding his hand, or without any special physical contact. When it can be done naturally, however, the laying on of hands adds a desirable dimension to our praying for healing.

Praying in tongues may also be used advantageously in praying for healing. We are sometimes unsure exactly what to pray for; we sometimes find ourselves at a loss for words to express the concerns of our heart. In these situations, those who have received the gift of tongues can augment their prayers for healing with prayers that go beyond their own words, but which are well understood by God (Rom. 8:26-27).

As in all aspects of the Christian life, we will need to learn and grow in our praying for healing. Maturity comes from experience. We should not be surprised if our first attempts at praying for healing appear to us to be halting and awkward. However, our prayers will probably seem much less awkward to the person we are praying for; they will sense our love and concern for them. And fortunately for us, God does not evaluate our prayers on the basis of eloquence, but on the basis of the desires of our hearts.

A study of the gospel accounts of the healing ministry of Jesus can help us learn to pray for healing. If we read the gospels with an eye to the many and varied instances in which Jesus healed someone, we will grow in our appreciation of this aspect of Jesus' work of redemption. Our confidence in praying for healing will grow accordingly.

We do not need to find a perfect formula for praying for healing; we simply need to turn to God for health. We do not need to be able to understand the mystery of suffering; we must simply trust in God whose love surpasses our understanding. There is no magic technique to be discovered and mastered, no hidden knowledge revealed only to a few. There is simply the need to pray, to ask, to trust to our limit. God can—and does—answer imperfect prayer and respond to even halting faith. He simply asks that we ask.

Our faith for healing should therefore be a peaceful faith. We are children turning to our Father. We do not need to strain to achieve more faith than we are capable of; we do not need to suppress our doubts by sheer willpower. Our faith should acknowledge that we are asking our Father to perform a work that is beyond our own power. Our faith should acknowledge that we do not fully understand the mystery of God's plan, and that we cannot control the outcome of our prayer. Our faith is simply our obedience to Jesus' invitation to us to pray, our confidence in Our Father's love for us, our placing ourselves in God's hands.

Our faith must realize that it is God's general

Faith for Healing 51

will that sickness be healed. We are not praying to convince God that he should heal; we are praying because we know he does want to heal. We are not praying to earn a healing; we are praying because Jesus Christ has won healing for us. We are not praying to a distant God who is disinterested in us; we are praying to a Father who loves us with an infinite love.

However, this does not mean that we will generally have certitude about the way our prayer will be answered. Unless we have received some specific message or direction from God, giving us a revelation of his will for a particular situation, we cannot be certain how our prayer will be answered. There is a faith in the healing power of God that all Christians should have—and there is a special gift of faith given to some, enabling them to pray with certitude that God intends to heal the person they are praying for. Unless God has given this special gift of faith, we cannot have utter certitude how our prayer will be answered—and we should not strain to have this certitude.

Some pray for healing for themselves or others—and then feel very guilty if the healing does not occur. They blame themselves for not having enough faith; they strain to have a faith free of all doubts, a certainty that God is going to heal them. Since it is virtually impossible to suppress doubts by sheer willpower, such people blame themsevles and their doubts for obstructing God's healing, and feel even more guilty.

Such a view of faith is misguided. Our faith must acknowledge our doubts at the same time that it places our trust in God; it must admit our ignorance of the details of God's plan for us at the same time it acknowledges that God's general will for us is that we be well. Our faith must acknowledge that healing depends upon God, not upon anything within our own powers. We cannot force a healing by our shouting or show of bravado; we can only ask our Father for health, peacefully secure in his love for us.

Francis MacNutt in his book *Healing* describes very succinctly the kind of faith we should have in praying for healing: "My faith is in God—not in my own faith."

> My faith opens up doubts once I begin to look at its quality. When a blind person, one who has no eyes whatsoever in the sockets, comes forward to ask for prayer, I wonder if I have the faith required for such a healing. Most of us would have to admit our doubts. Once we begin to look at our faith, however, rather than at God, we begin to concentrate on our own inadequacy.

The way, then, to pray in faith is to turn to God in complete trust that he knows what is

Faith for Healing 53

best, that he loves us more than anyone else, and that he has the power to accomplish whatever we need; to accept our doubts about our own adequacy and our prediction of results as normal; to see that the faith-action we need to take is to pray for the sick; and to leave the results up to God.

Healing is a mystery. Even those most gifted in a healing ministry today admit that they do not know why God heals some people and not others. We will not resolve this mystery by trying to impose our own rules on God. Rather, our faith for healing must mean that we enter willingly into this mystery, wanting to be healed because we know that God's plan is for man to be healthy, praying for healing because Jesus invited us to, trusting God for healing because we believe that he loves us with a Father's love—and consigning the outcome to his will and wisdom.

5

RESURRECTION

I think that what we suffer in this life can never be compared to the glory, as yet unrevealed, which is waiting for us. The whole creation is eagerly waiting for God to reveal his sons. It was not for any fault on the part of creation that it was made unable to attain its purpose, it was made so by God; but creation still retains the hope of being freed, like us, from its slavery to decadence, to enjoy the same freedom and glory as the children of God. From the beginning till now the entire creation, as we know, has been groaning in

Resurrection

one great act of giving birth; and not only creation, but all of us who possess the firstfruits of the Spirit, we too groan inwardly as we wait for our bodies to be set free. For we must be content to hope that we shall be saved—our salvation is not in sight, we should not have to be hoping for it if it were—but, as I say, we must hope to be saved since we are not saved yet—it is something we must wait for with patience.

Rom. 8:18-25

Jesus Christ came to bring us abundant life. He came to heal us of the effects of sin, and restore to us the splendor of being made in the image and likeness of God himself. This book was written in the belief that Jesus' healing of the sick was an integral part of his mission on earth, and remains a work of his today.

But despite the awesome power of Jesus' works of healing, there was an incompleteness to his earthly ministry. There is no evidence that those whom Jesus healed never fell sick again; there is no evidence that they were given an immunity to disease and suffering. If Jesus had bestowed such a gift upon them, surely some mention of it would have been made in the New Testament. We can only assume, for example, that Peter's mother-in-law, once cured by Jesus, was nevertheless thereafter still prone to the sicknesses that normally afflict mankind.

Even the most awesome of Jesus' healings—raising the dead back to life—did not give perfect life. Lazarus died again. Lazarus, freed once from the bonds of death by the power of Jesus Christ, was still subject to the common sentence of humanity, that to each is appointed a time to die. The somber words of Ecclesiastes still held sway, even for those Jesus raised from the dead: There is "a time for giving birth, a time for dying" (Eccles. 3:2).

The miracles worked by the followers of Jesus in his name likewise did not grant perfect health, immunity from disease, or a prepayment of death's obligations. Paul cured the sick—but was sick himself. Paul raised the dead back to life—but died himself. Those that Paul raised once back to life still had to pass from this life by way of death again. There was an awesomeness to the miracles worked by Paul, but also an incompleteness.

In the face of continuing sickness, in the face of eventual death—even for the most devoted followers of Jesus—what do the words and promises of Jesus mean? He said, "I have come so that they may have life and have it to the full" (John 10:10). He said, "I tell you most solemnly, whoever listens to my words and believes in the one who sent me, has eternal life" (John 5:24). He said "Ask, and you will receive" (Luke 11:9). Are these empty exaggerations, rhetorical promises?

Resurrection

A servant is not greater than his master, nor a disciple than his teacher. Jesus invites those who acknowledge his Lordship to follow in his footsteps. The path that Jesus followed led to Calvary—and resurrection. Those who would be disciples of Jesus are called to follow after him.

Why was it ordained that the life of Jesus lead to Calvary? Why was not salvation won for mankind by some other means? We do not know. Ultimately, it is a mystery why God chose the death and resurrection of his son to free man from the death that sin had earned. Ultimately, we are simply confronted with the fact: through Calvary we have been given salvation. "The language of the cross may be illogical to those who are not on the way to salvation, but those of us who are on the way see it as God's power to save" (1 Cor. 1:18).

We also cannot understand why the salvation we have been granted does not take effect in us completely and immediately. Why must we still face death and sickness, suffering and sadness? In his sovereign power, God could have designed a plan of salvation that granted us complete victory over sickness and death here and now, a plan giving us the innocence to walk with him as Adam walked with God in Eden. But that was not God's plan of salvation for us. "We must be content to hope that we shall be saved—our salvation is not in sight, we should not have to be hoping for it if it were—but, as I say, we must hope to be saved since we are not saved yet—it is something we must wait for with patience" (Rom. 8:24-25).

The full promise of Jesus Christ is a promise of resurrection to eternal life. "It is my Father's will that whoever sees the Son and believes in him shall have eternal life, and that I shall raise him up on the last day .... Anyone who does eat my flesh and drink my blood has eternal life, and I shall raise him up on the last day" (John 6:40, 54). Jesus Christ gives us eternal life, beginning here and now—but an eternal life that is only fully manifested on the last day, through resurrection.

The account in John's Gospel of the raising of Lazarus teaches us about resurrection and eternal life—God's gifts to us out of his love for us. Jesus expresses his deep love for his friend Lazarus when he meets Mary, the dead man's sister: "At the sight of her tears, and those of the Jews who followed her, Jesus said in great distress, with a sigh that came straight from the heart, 'Where have you put him?' They said, 'Lord, come and see.' Jesus wept, and the Jews said, 'See how much he loved him!'" (John 11: 33-36).

Jesus was concerned that his friend Lazarus had died; he was concerned about the sorrow this death brought to the family and friends of

Lazarus; he was sorrowful himself that death should have claimed someone he loved. "Jesus wept." "See how much he loved him."

Seeing the love of Jesus for Lazarus, some of those present asked a very natural question: "He opened the eyes of the blind man, could he not have prevented this man's death?" (John 11:37). If Jesus had the power to preserve those he loved from suffering and death, why did he not use it? If God is almighty and loving, why does he allow sickness to afflict mankind?

Such questions require God to conform to our understanding and expectations. We want God to act the way we would act. We want Jesus to vindicate himself according to our standards. Our demands are a faint echo of the temptations Jesus faced in the wilderness: "The tempter came and said to him, 'If you are the Son of God, tell these stones to turn into loaves . . . If you are the Son of God, throw yourself down'" from the parapet of the Temple (Matt. 4:3, 6). *If* you are the Son of God, work the signs we demand. *If* you are the Son of God, banish all suffering.

Our questions also resemble the accusations put to Jesus on the cross: "He saved others, let him save himself if he is the Christ of God, the chosen one" (Luke 23:35). "Let him come down from the cross now, and we will believe in him. He puts his trust in God; now let God rescue him if he wants him" (Matt. 27:42-43). Did not Jesus have the power to come down from the cross? Did not the Father love Jesus? The ultimate question about suffering and death is not why God allows it to be present in the world, but why God ordained that we were to be given life through the suffering and death of his son Jesus. Our wisdom can no more comprehend this mystery than the wisdom of Job could fathom his own suffering. Like Isaiah, we must finally confess that the thoughts of God are as high above the understanding of man as the heavens are above the earth (Isa. 55:9).

Mary and Martha, the sisters of Lazarus, could not understand the ways of God either. When Lazarus was stricken with illness, they sent Jesus the message, "Lord, the man you love is ill" (John 11:3). Contrary to their expectations, however, Jesus did not come to heal Lazarus, and Lazarus died.

Later, when Martha heard that Jesus was finally coming, she ran out to greet him. She did not understand why Jesus had allowed his friend to die. She believed that Jesus could have healed him if he had come in time, and she did have confidence that the Father would honor any prayer of Jesus: "If you had been here, my brother would not have died, but I know that, even now, whatever you ask of God, he will grant you" (John 11:21-22). Mary, her sister, will later echo her words: "Mary went to Jesus, and as soon as she saw him she threw herself at his feet, saying, 'Lord, if you had been here, my brother would not have died" (John 11:32).

Jesus responded to Martha's faith—to acknowledge it and increase it: "Your brother will rise again" (John 11:23). Martha was reluctant to accept a literal, immediate meaning to these words. She could only profess a belief shared by many Jews at that time—that there would be an eventual resurrection of the dead. "I know he will rise again at the resurrection on the last day" (John 11:24).

Jesus then made one of the boldest claims recorded in the gospels: "I am the resurrection and the life. If anyone believes in me, even though he dies he will live, and whoever lives and believes in me will never die" (John 11:25).

Jesus Christ himself claimed to be the resurrection promised to man; he claimed that eternal life was to be found in him and through him. Resurrection is not merely something we will experience on the last day, at the end of the world; eternal life begins when we enter into a relationship with Jesus. The life that Jesus gives cannot be taken away even by the event of our death. The eternal life that Jesus gives begins here and now, and blossoms into fullness after death. Jesus Christ is our resurrection, not because he will bring us back to life after we die, but because he gives us life that will endure through death. In him we will never die.

Martha was given the grace to understand Jesus' blunt claim. "Do you believe this?" "Yes Lord, I believe that you are the Christ, the Son of God, the one who has to come into this world" (John 11:26-27). Martha realized that Jesus was talking less about his power to bring dead men back to life than about himself and his identity. Martha's profession of faith is therefore a profession of her faith that Jesus is the Christ, the Son of God, the promised redeemer. That is the essential truth. Jesus' power over life and death is secondary, and flows from his being the Son of God.

Martha grasped the important fact, and placed her faith in Jesus. This did not mean that she understood in advance how Jesus was to manifest his power. Later, when Jesus asked that the stone blocking the tomb of Lazarus be removed, it was Martha who protested that it was the fourth day since burial, and "by now he will smell" (John 11:39). How human of her to accept Jesus as the Son of God and trust him for eternal life—but worry about his power over odors!

The full meaning of Jesus' words to his disciples before they traveled to Bethany is now apparent: "Lazarus is dead; and for your sake I am glad I was not there because now you will believe" (John 11:15). The death of Lazarus provided Jesus with the opportunity to raise him back to life—a miracle that confirmed the faith of his followers. But the raising of Lazarus also provided the setting for Jesus' claim "I am the resurrection and the life," and for a faith response: "I believe that you are the Christ, the Son of God." Jesus raised Lazarus from the dead for the sake of his followers' belief—for their belief in him as the Son of God.

Our belief in the healing power of Jesus must be a belief in him as the one who gives eternal life—nothing less. Jesus is not someone who merely takes away the aches and pains of our earthly life; he gives us eternal life. Jesus does not simply give us an indefinite extension of life here and now, postponing death; he gives us life that endures through death.

Therefore Paul coud say, "I think that what we suffer in this life can never be compared to the glory as yet unrevealed, which is waiting for us" (Rom. 8:18). Paul acknowledged that there is suffering: being a follower of Christ does not give one immunity to pain. At the same time, there is a glory that is awaiting us. And it is a glory that we are beginning to participate in now, by way of foretaste. We have been given the "first-fruits of the Spirit" (Rom. 8:23). Eternal life begins for us now, even if we shall only experience it in fullness after death.

It is in this context that we pray for healing from sickness and injury. It is in this context that we turn to God in our suffering, and turn our suffering over to him. We pray for a first taste of the glory that is to be revealed.

Despite having the first-fruits of the Spirit, we "groan inwardly as we wait for our bodies to be set free" (Rom. 8:23). We must await our full redemption with patience; we must await God's power to grant us resurrection. But we wait in hope: we have been granted in Jesus Christ a foretaste of the life that awaits us. We are given healing of our body, as a first fruit of the harvest that is promised us:

> Then I saw a new heaven and a new earth; for the first heaven and the first earth had passed away, and the sea was no more. And I saw the holy city, new Jerusalem, coming down out of heaven from God, prepared as a bride adorned for her husband; and I heard a great voice from the throne saying, "Behold, the dwelling of God is with men. He will dwell with them, and they shall be his people, and God himself will be with them; he will wipe away every tear from their eyes, and death shall be no more, neither shall there be mourning nor crying nor pain any more, for the former things have passed away."
>
> Rev. 21:1-4